Tatting
Patterns and Designs

Gun Blomqvist
and
Elwy Persson

Dover Publications, Inc., *New York*

Published in Canada by General Publishing Company, Ltd., 30 Lesmill Road, Don Mills, Toronto, Ontario.
Published in the United Kingdom by Constable and Company, Ltd.

This Dover edition, first published in 1988, is a slightly abridged republication of *Tatting: Patterns and Designs*, published by Van Nostrand Reinhold Company, New York, in 1974. (This book was originally published in Swedish under the title *Frivoliteter* by LTs förlag, Sweden.) It was translated from the Swedish by Marianne Turner. In the Dover edition, the section "Suppliers" has been omitted.

Manufactured in the United States of America
Dover Publications, Inc., 31 East 2nd Street, Mineola, N.Y. 11501

Library of Congress Cataloging-in-Publication Data

Blomqvist, Gun, 1933–
 [Frivoliteter. English]
 Tatting patterns and designs / by Gun Blomqvist and Elwy Persson.
      p.   cm.
 Translation of: Frivoliteter.
 "A slightly abridged republication of Tatting . . . published by Van Nostrand Reinhold Company, New York, in 1974"—T.p. verso.
 ISBN 0-486-25813-0 (pbk.)
 1. Tatting—Patterns.   I. Persson, Elwy.   II. Title.
 TT840.T38B5713   1988
 746.43′6—dc19   88-20305
                                                                              CIP

Contents

Introduction

Tatting is a type of knotted lace, made from cotton or linen thread with a shuttle.

Historians are divided as to the origins of tatting. Some maintain that tatting began in France since the word for tatting in several languages (e.g. in Scandinavia – *frivoliteter*) seems to be derived from the French for lace, *frivolité*. Some theories make Italy the country of origin, others Germany.

One of the earliest records that we do have is the 'The Royal Tatter', a poem by the English poet Sir Charles Sedley in 1707. The central figure in the poem is Queen Mary II (1662–1694) who is described at her homely pastime of tatting. This means that the craft must have existed at least as early as the seventeenth century.

Tatting reached a height in popularity in European countries in the second half of the eighteenth century. It appears to have been a craft which the ladies of rank especially enjoyed as it is easy and graceful. There are several portraits from the period showing ladies engaged in tatting.

It is true to say though that their work is unlikely to have been as fine as today's. This is not due to any lack of skill but because the shuttles they used were cumbersome and the yarn consequently coarse. However, the shuttles were richly ornamented and were made of materials varying from gold to ivory, mother-of-pearl to turtle shell. Some were delicately painted while others inlaid with precious stones.

Fig. 1–4 shows a few examples of such shuttles. The one top left is made of mother-of-pearl, with the crest of a distinguished Swedish family (the Mannerheims) on one side. The initials JEM on the other side probably belonged to a daughter of the Mannerheims – Johanna Elisabeth – who lived in the eighteenth century.

Interest in tatting lapsed from the end of the eighteenth century until the mid-nineteenth century. European fashion magazines were largely responsible for the revival. They began to restore enthusiasm by printing descriptions of tatting techniques, offering guidance, and even arranging competitions.

People worked with great liveliness and imagination and produced articles which were both useful and ornamental. These included lace for the handkerchiefs, underwear, children's clothes, and collars as well as a variety of small squares and round pieces for inserting into cushions, handbags, and table cloths.

This revival only lasted until the early 1870's. Once again the coarseness of the materials seems largely to account for the decline in interest.

Not until the 1920's did tatting regain its popularity. Materials had improved by this time and the shuttles were more manageable. Also a great number of

Fig. I-1. Queen Charlotte and her daughter, *painted by the eighteenth century artist Benjamin West. The picture hangs in St. James's Palace, London. Copyright reserved.*

Fig. I-2. Madame Adelaide, *daughter of Louis XV, painted by Jean–Marc Nattier (1685-1766). It hangs in the Palace of Versailles.*

Fig. I-3. The Duchess of Albemarle, *painted by Sir Joshua Reynolds (1723-1792). Reproduced by courtesy of the National Gallery, London.*

I-2.

I-3.

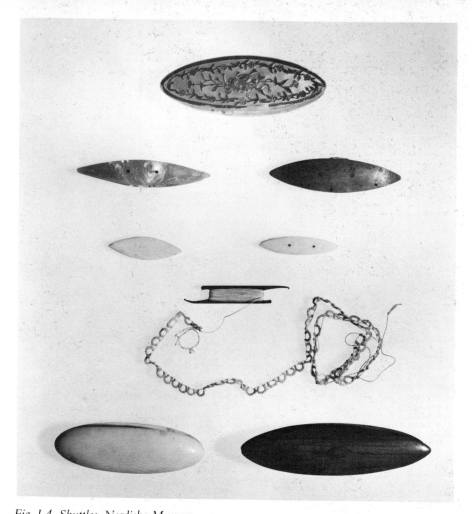

Fig. I-4. Shuttles. Nordiska Museum.
Fig. I-5. Handkerchiefs with tatted lace, made around 1900. Nordiska Museum.
The inscription at the top of Fig. I-5 reads as follows: EMILIA HOFFMAN,
SWEDEN; TATTED WORK AFTER HER OWN DESIGN. AWARDED
PRIZES AT SEVERAL EXHIBITIONS

pattern books appeared on the market at the time containing an attractive
balance of old and new designs.

Now, after 50 years, the craft is being revived again. It is this renewed interest
which has prompted us to prepare this book. We hope that the numerous
patterns will serve two purposes – to encourage those who have little or no
experience of tatting (and we have included a chapter on basic techniques to
help) and to give inspiration to those who know the craft and who are looking
for new ideas.

I-5.

I-6.

1. Tools & Materials

The most important tool for tatting is a shuttle. A shuttle should be about 7cm. (2in.) long and 2cm. ($\frac{3}{4}$in.) wide, and made of celluloid, bone, tortoise shell, or plastic. It is made up of two tapering discs held together by a middle section called a bobbin. The tips of the discs should touch at both ends to keep the thread from getting loose unintentionally. There is a hole in the middle of the bobbin for threading the yarn. The yarn is pushed through the hole, wound round the bobbin of the shuttle until it reaches the outer edge. Make sure the shuttle is not too full, or the yarn will tend to get dirty and be harder to work with.

It is a good idea to have more than one shuttle on hand so that you can try out several patterns at the same time.

In more advanced work requiring two shuttles, it is helpful if the shuttles are different in colour as the two seperate yarns can then be easily distinguished.

You will get the best results if you use an even, fine yarn, one with neither too loose nor too tight a twist. This kind of yarn is easy to work with.

D.M.C. Cordonnet Special is very good and is available in many different thicknesses and colours. The gauge numbers given in the instructions can, of course, be varied for coarser or finer yarns, as required. When considering what thickness the yarn should be, take into account the size of the finished article and the intricacy of the motif. As a general rule thicker yarns will suit bigger motifs, smaller yarns more delicate patterns.

We have tried out various other materials, such as window blind cord, fishing net twine, and rug warp, in an effort to produce a coarse, rustic effect, but these have proved uncomfortable to handle and difficult to work with. After all, the most delightful quality of tatting is its delicacy!

2. Techniques

Tatting consists of stitches and picots. The most common stitch is the 'double stitch'. Picots are loops made by leaving a distance between double stitches, and it is important for both practical as well as aesthetic reasons that these be even. For this reason it is important to learn how to handle the shuttle evenly, without any jerking movements.

Joining Rings

When the required number of rings have been made, lift the work round your thumb. Join in the required picot. Both threads must be on the underside of the work.

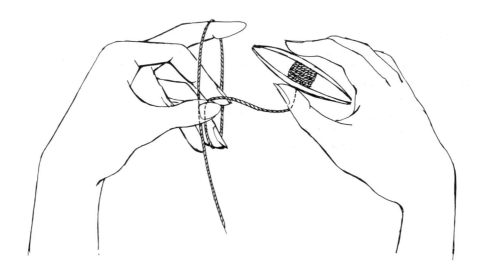

Fig. 2-1. The starting position – hold the shuttle in the right hand with the thread passed round the left.

Fig. 2-2. Pass the shuttle in the direction of the arrow, through the loop of thread in the left hand. Tighten the thread, at the same time closing the fingers of the left hand on the knot. A half-stitch has now been formed.

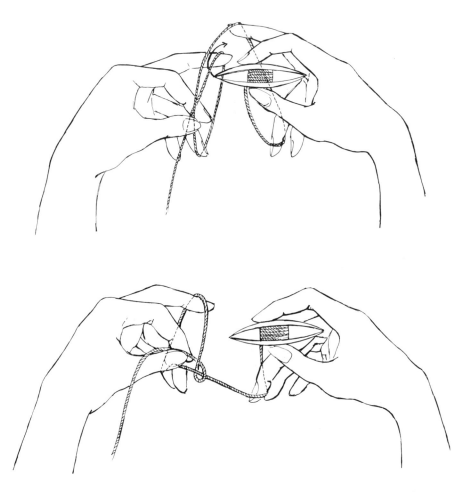

Fig. 2-3. Tighten the stitch by again extending the fingers of the left hand. Hold it with the thumb and forefinger of the left hand. Note that the shuttle thread must always be kept tight.

Fig. 2-4. The second part of the double stitch. The index finger of the right hand pulls the thread down, and the shuttle is passed through the loop from the back to the front in the direction of the arrow. Tighten as before. It is also possible to let the shuttle thread hang and to work as in the sketch.

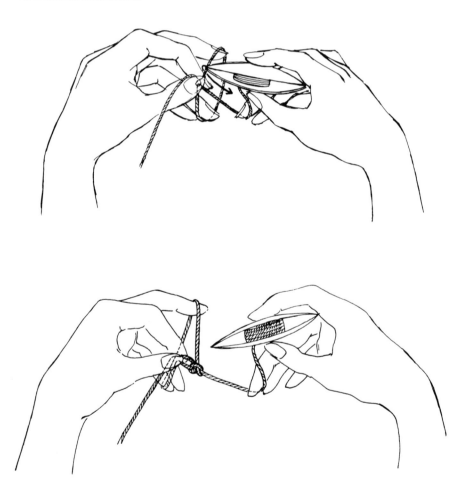

Fig. 2-5. Completed double stitch.

Fig. 2-6. Picots. These are obtained by leaving a loop of the thread between two stitches. The picot forms through the closing of the double stitches – naturally it is necessary to ensure that all the picots are of the same length.

Fig. 2-7. Joining of rings. This is done with a crochet hook.

Joining Threads

Make a weaver's knot (see Fig. 2–8). The join can be made either between two rings or onto the thread which is round the hand. The join should be positioned so that it is hidden by the stitches.

Second Thread from Ball

Make the double stitch of the first ring as usual, tucking in the end and letting it follow the shuttle thread a short distance. When the ring has been completed, make the chain, which requires a second thread, by reversing the work under the ring and round the hand. Proceed as for the first ring. When the chain has been completed, bring the double stitches together, reverse the work, make the next ring and join it to the first.

Fig. 2-8. A sketch showing the two methods of making a weaver's knot.

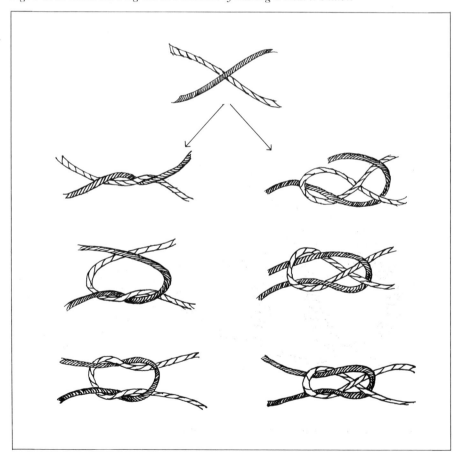

Two Shuttles
The second thread must be on a shuttle when parts of the chain do not face in the opposite direction to the ring. Two shuttles must also be used for working designs.

Definition of Terms
Inner ring – the middle portion of the work.
Ring – the section of the pattern which is always tightened so that a separate unit is formed.
Chain – a section of the pattern where the beginning and end are connected.
Josephine knot – a section of the pattern consisting of half stitches. The beginning and end do not quite join.
Half stitch – the first half of a double stitch.
Picot – a loop between double stitches.

A middle ring consisting, for instance, of 2×12, will theoretically contain only eleven picots, but actually it must have twelve. The twelfth one is worked by tying the two ends together to form a picot.

Nature as a Model
When you have mastered the technique, you will want to create your own patterns. Nature is full of things to inspire the tatter, such as seed capsules, leaves, flowers, dry twigs, mosses, and any number of things. See if the pictures on pages 20, 31, 52, 73 and 88 can't suggest something to you.

3. Edgings & Insertions

13 Patterns (pages 21 – 30)

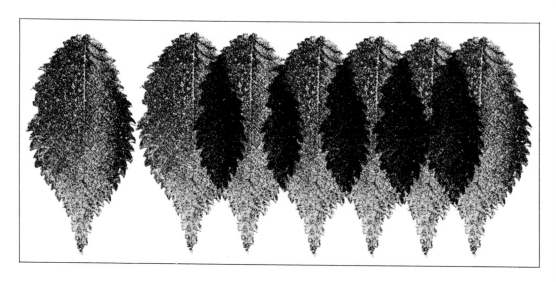

Gullan

Purpose: Edging
Yarn: D.M.C. No. 80
Size: 0·7 cm. ($\frac{1}{8}$ in.) wide
Abbreviations: Number = number of double stitches between the picots,
   R = ring, + = joining, — = picot.
Number of shuttles: One

R 5 — 5 — 5 — 5. R 5 + 5 — 5 — 5.
Repeat until the lace is the required length.

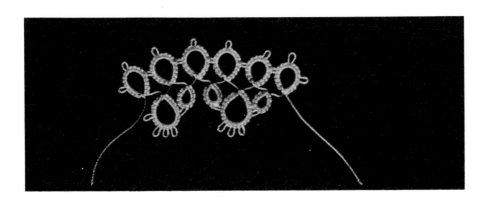

Inga

Purpose: Edging
Yarn. D.M.C. No. 30
Size: 2 cm. ($\frac{7}{8}$ in.) wide
Abbreviations: Number = number of double stitches between the picots,
   R = ring, + = joining, — = picot
Number of shuttles: One

R 5 — 5 — 5 — 5. R 6 — 6. R 5 + 5 — 5 — 5. R 6 + 4 — 2 — 2 — 4 — 6.
  R 5 + 5 — 5 — 5. R 6 + 6.
Repeat until the lace is the required length.

Ulla

Purpose: Edging or insertion

Yarn: D.M.C. No. 30

Size: 1·4 cm. ($\frac{5}{8}$ in.) wide

Abbreviations: Number = number of double stitches between the picots, R = ring, C = chain, × = joining, — = picot

Number of shuttles: One, and second thread

R 5 — 5 — 5 — 5. C 5 — 5. R 5 + 5 — 5 — 5. C 5 — 5. R 5 + 5 — 5 — 5.
Repeat until the lace is the required length.

Astrid

Purpose: Edging

Yarn: D.M.C. 30

Size: 3 cm. (1$\frac{3}{8}$ in.) wide

Abbreviations: Number = number of double stitches between the picots, R = ring, C = chain, + = joining, — = picot

Number of shuttles: One, and second thread

R 5 — 3 — 3 — 3 — 3 — 3 — 5. R 5 + 3 — 3 — 3 — 3 — 3 — 5.
R 5 + 3 — 3 — 3 — 3 — 3 — 5. C 5 — 5 — 3 — 3 — 5 — 5 +. C 5 — 5.
R 5 + 5 — 5. C 5. R 5 + 3 — 3 — 3 — 3 — 5.
R 5 + 3 — 3 — 3 — 3 — 3 — 5. R 5 + 3 — 3 — 3 — 3 — 5. C 5.
R 5 + 5 — 5. C 5 + 5 +. C 5 + 5 — 3 — 3 — 5 — 5.

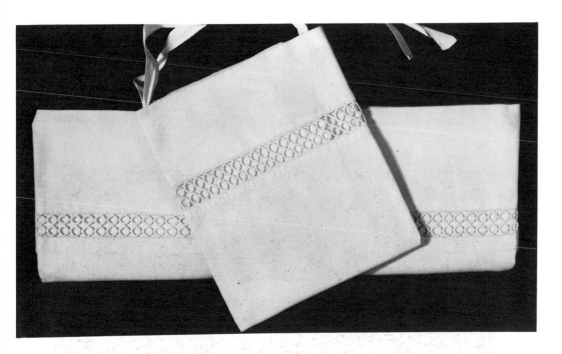

Fia

Purpose: Insertion

Yarn: D.M.C. No. 20

Size: 2 cm. ($\frac{3}{4}$ in.) wide

Abbreviations: Number = number of double stitches between the picots,
    R = ring, C = chain, + = joining, — = picot

Number of shuttles: One

Row 1: R 5 — 5 — 5 — 5.   C 7.   R 5 + 5 — 5 — 5.   C 7.
Repeat until the lace is the required length.
Row 2: R 5 — 5 + 5 — 5.   C 7.   R 5 + 5 + 5 — 5.   C 7.

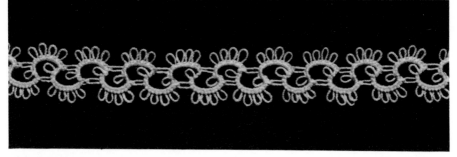

Ingeborg

Purpose: Edging or insertion

Yarn: D.M.C. No. 30

Size: 1 cm. ($\frac{3}{8}$ in.) wide

Abbreviations: Number = number of double stitches between the picots, C = chain, — = picot

Number of shuttles: One, and second thread.

C2 — 2 — 2 — 2 — 2 — 2 — 2.   Reverse work.
C2 — 2 — 2 — 2 — 2 — 2 — 2.

Join to the picot first made.

Repeat until the lace is the required length.

Martha

Purpose: Edging

Yarn: D.M.C. No. 30

Size: 1·5 cm. ($\frac{5}{8}$ in.) wide

Abbreviations: Number = number of double stitches between the picots, R = ring, C = chain, + = joining, 2 × 6 = 2—2—2—2—2—2, — = picot

Number of shuttles: One, and second thread

Row 1: R 6—5—1. R 1 + 5—5—1. R 1 + 5—6. C 16. R 6 + 5—1.
R 1 + 5—5—1. R 1 + 5—6. C 16.

Repeat until the lace is the required length.

Row 2: + C 2—4—2 × 7—4—2 + 4. C 2 + 4—2 × 7—4—2 +.

Carla

Purpose: Edging

Yarn: D.M.C. No. 30

Size: 2 cm. ($\frac{7}{8}$ in.) wide

Abbreviations: Number = number of double stitches between the picots, R = ring, C = chain, + = joining, — = picot

Number of shuttles: One, and second thread

Row 1: R 4—4—4—4. C 5—5. R 4 + 6—6—4. C 5—5.
R 4 + 4—4—4. C 5—5. R 4 + 6—6—4.

Repeat until the lace is the required length.

Row 2: + C 2—9—9—2 +. C 2 + 9—9—2 +.

Boel

Purpose: Edging

Yarn: D.M.C. No. 30

Size: 4 cm. ($1\frac{5}{8}$ in.) wide

Abbreviations: Number = number of double stitches between the picots,
R = ring, C = chain, + = joining, $3 \times 7 = 3 - 3 - 3 - 3 - 3 - 3 - 3$,
— = picot

Number of shuttles: One, and second thread

Motif 1: Three-leaved clover: R5—2—2—2—2—5.
R5+2—2—2—2—5.   R5+2—2—2—2—5.   C5—2—2—5.
R5+4—4—4—4—5.   C8.
Three-leaved clover: R5+2—2—2—2—5.   R5+2—2—2—2—5.
R5+2—2—2—2—5.   C8.   R5+4—4—4—4—5.
C5+2+2+5.
Three-leaved clover: R5—2—2+2—2—5.   R5+2—2—2—2—5.
R5+2—2—2—2—5.   C5—3 × 7—5+.   C5—3 × 7—5.

Motif 2 and all subsequent motifs: Same as motif 1 except that the chains in the
upper edge are joined, as the illustration shows.

Selma

Purpose: Insertion

Yarn: D.M.C. No. 30

Size: 4·5 cm. (1¾ in.) wide

Abbreviations: Number = number of double stitches between the picots, R = ring, C = chain, Hs = half stitch, 2 × 6 = 2 — 2 — 2 — 2 — 2 — 2, — = picot

Number of shuttles: One, and second thread

Row 1: R 3 × 12. C 2 × 6. R 5 — 5. C 2 × 6. R 5 — 5. C 2 × 6. R 3 × 12.

Row 2: 8 Hs. 8 Hs. R 5 + 5. R 5 — 5. 8 Hs. 8 Hs. R 3 — 3 — 3 — 3 — 3 — 3 + 3 — 3 — 3 — 3 — 3 — 3. R 3 — 3 — 3 — 3 — 3 — 3 + 3 — 3 — 3 — 3 — 3 — 3. R 3 × 12. R 3 × 12. 8 Hs. 8 Hs. R 5 + 5. R 5 — 5. 8 Hs. 8 Hs. R 3 — 3 — 3 — 3 — 3 — 3 + 3 — 3 — 3 — 3 — 3 — 3. R 3 × 12. R 3 × 12.

Row 3: Same as row 1 but joined, as the illustration shows.

27

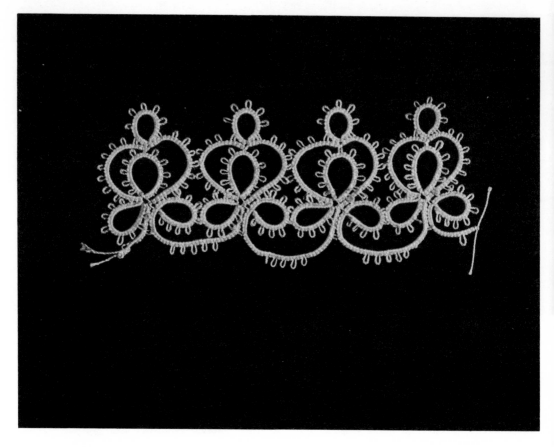

Annette

Purpose: Edging

Yarn: D.M.C. No. 40

Size: 3·5 cm. (1⅜ in.) wide

Abbreviations: Number = number of double stitches between the picots,
R = ring, C = chain, + = joining, 3 × 8 = 3 — 3 — 3 — 3 — 3 — 3 — 3 — 3,
— = picot

Number of shuttles: Two

Shuttle 1: R 3 × 10.

Shuttle 2: R 3 × 12.   C 3 + 3 × 9 +.

Shuttle 1: R 3 + 3 × 7.

Shuttle 2: C 3 + 3 × 9 +.

Shuttle 1: R 3 + 3 × 9.   C 7 + 7 — 3 — 3 — 3 — 3 — 7 — 7.

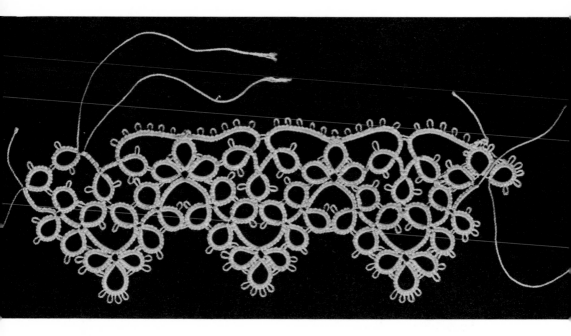

Margareta

Purpose: Edging

Yarn: D.M.C. No. 30

Size: 5 cm. (2 in.) wide

Abbreviations: Number = number of double stitches between the picots, R = ring, C = chain, + = joining, — = picot

Number of shuttles: Two

Row 1: Shuttle 1: R 5 — 5 — 5 — 5. R 5 + 5 — 2 — 5 — 5. R 5 + 5 — 5 — 5.

   Shuttle 2: C 10. R 5 — 5 — 5 — 5.

   Shuttle 1: R 5 + 5 — 5 — 5. C 5. R 5 + 5 — 5 — 5.

   Shuttle 2: R 5 + 5 — 5 — 5.

   Shuttle 1: C 10.

   Shuttle 2: R 5 + 3 — 2 — 3 — 5. R 5 + 3 — 2 — 2 — 2 — 3 — 5.

   R 5 + 3 — 2 — 3 — 5.

   Shuttle 1: C 10. R 5 — 5 + 5 — 5.

   Shuttle 2: R 5 + 5 — 5 — 5.

   Shuttle 1: C 5. R 5 + 5 — 5 — 5.

   Shuttle 2: R 5 + 5 — 5 — 5. C 10. Repeat Row 1.

Row 2: Attach thread to bottom ring.

   + C 1 — 1 + 3 — 3 — 3 — 3 — 3 — 3 — 5.

   R 5 — 5 + 5 — 5. C 5. R 5 — 5 + 5 — 5. C 5. R 5 — 5 + 5 — 5.

   C 5 + 3 — 3 — 3 — 3 — 3 — 3 + 1 — 1 +.

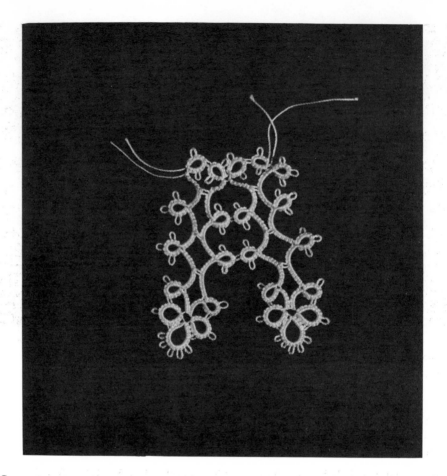

Svea

Purpose: Edging. Can also be used for collar

Yarn: D.M.C. No 30

Size: 5 cm. (2 in.) wide

Abbreviations: Number = number of double stitches between the picots,
   R = ring, C = chain, $2 \times 6 = 2 - 2 - 2 - 2 - 2 - 2$, — = picot

Number of shuttles: One, and second thread

Motif 1: R 3 — 3 — 3 — 3. R 3 — 3 — 3 — 3. C 6 — 6. R 3 — 3 — 3 — 3.
   C 6 — 6. R 3 — 3 — 3 — 3. C 6 — 6. R 4 — 4 — 4. C 6.
   R 4 + 4 — 4 — 4. R 4 + 2 × 6 — 4. R 4 + 4 — 4 — 4. C 6. R 4 — 4 — 4.
   C 6 + 6. R 3 — 3 — 3 — 3. C 6 + 6. R 3 — 3 — 3 — 3. C 6 + 6.
   R 3 — 3 + 3 — 3. R 3 — 3 — 3 — 3. C 6 — 6.

Motif 2 and all subsequent motifs: The same as 1.

4. Stars

45 Patterns (pages 33–51)
Mounting of Mobile (page 32)

Mounting a mobile requires four brass wires, 17, 13, 11 and 9 cm. ($6\frac{3}{4}$, $5\frac{1}{4}$, $4\frac{3}{8}$ and $3\frac{1}{2}$ in.) long, respectively. The length of the yarn to link the wires has to be worked out so that the motifs hang freely and balance correctly.

Purpose: For mobile, table-cloth or handkerchief insertions
Yarn: D.M.C. No. 30
Size: 6·5 cm. (2⅝ in.), 5 cm. (2 in.), 4 cm. (1⅝ in.), 3·5 cm. (1⅜ in.), 2 cm. (¾ in.)
Abbreviations: Number = number of double stitches between the picots,
Ir = inner ring, R = ring, C = chain, + = joining, +— = joining and picot,
3 × 4 = 3 — 3 — 3 — 3, — = picot

Star No. 1. Two Shuttles
Row 1: Shuttle 1: R 4 — 4 — 5 — 5. C 6 + — 6. Repeat 5 times.
Row 2: C 8 + (shuttle 2: R 6 — 6) 8 + — 8 + (shuttle 2: R 6 — 6) 8 +.
Row 3: C 6 — 6 — 6 — 6 — 6 — 6 — 6 +. C 6 + 6 — 6 — 6 — 6 — 6 — 6.
Row 4: C + 6 + — 8 + — 8 + — 8 + — 6 +.
Row 5: C 6 + (shuttle 2: R 6 — 6) 10 + (shuttle 2: R 6 — 6) 10 + (shuttle 2:
R 6 — 6) 10 + (shuttle 2: R 6 — 6) 6 +.

Star No. 2. One Shuttle and Second Thread
Ir: 5 × 5. Tie ends for fifth picot and cut.
  R 2 — 2 — 2 + 2 — 2 — 2. C 5. R 2 × 11. C 3 × 4. R 4 + 4. C 3 × 6.
  R 4 + 4. C 3 × 4 + 5. C 5.
  Repeat 5 times.

Star No. 3. Two Shuttles
Shuttle 1: R 5 — 5 — 5 — 5 (middle).
Shuttle 2: R 5 — 10 — 5.
Shuttle 1: C 11.
Shuttle 2: R 6 + 3 — 3 — 3 — 6. R 6 + 3 — 3 — 3 — 3 — 3 — 3 — 6.
  R 6 + 3 — 3 — 3 — 6.
Shuttle 1: C 11.
Repeat 4 times.

Star No. 4. One Shuttle and Second Thread
R 6 — 6. C 3 × 7. R 6 + 6. C 3 × 5. R 6 + 6. C 3 × 5. R 6 + 6.
  C 3 × 5 +. C 3 × 4. R 6 + 6. C 3 × 4. R 6 + 6. C 3 × 4. R 6 + 6.
  C 3 × 4. R 6 + 6. C 3 × 4. R 6 + 6. C 3 × 4. R 6 + 6. C 3 × 4.

Star No. 5. Tie Shuttle and Second Threads Together.
C 3 × 7. R 3 × 12. R 3 + 3 × 11. C 3 + 3 × 6.

35

Purpose: For mobile, table-cloth or handkerchief insertions

Yarn: D.M.C. No. 30

Size: 5·5 cm. (2¼ in.), 5·5 cm. (2¼ in.), 4 cm. (1⅝ in.), 3 cm. (1¼ in.), 2 cm. (⅞ in.)

Abbreviations: Number = number of double stitches between the picots, Ir = inner ring, R = ring, C = chain, Jk = Josephine knot, Hs = half stitch, + = joining, 2 × 6 = 2—2—2—2—2—2, — = picot

Star No. 1. One Shuttle

Row 1: R 5—3—2—2—2—2—3—5. Jk 8 Hs.

  R 5 + 3—2—2—2—2—3—5. Jk 8 Hs. Repeat 4 times.

  Tie threads together and cut.

Row 2: R 2 + 2. R 5—3—2—2—2—2—3—5. Repeat 18 times.

Star No. 2. Two Shuttles

Ir: 4 × 8. Tie together for eighth picot and cut.

Shuttle 1: Three-leaved clover: R 5—3—3—3—5.

  R 5 + 3—3—3—3—5. R 5 + 3—3—3—5.

  C 10 (shuttle 2: R 6 + 6) 10.

Repeat 8 times.

Star No. 3. One Shuttle and Second Thread

R 2 × 8. C 3 × 7 +. R 2 × 8. C 3 + 3 × 6 +. Repeat as required.

The mobile star has 9 motifs.

Star No. 4. Two Shuttles

Shuttle 1: R 6—6.

Shuttle 2: Three-leaved clover: R 6—3—3—3—4.

  R 4 + 3—3—3—3—3—3—4.

  R 4 + 3—3—3—6.

Shuttle 1: C 10. R 6 + 6.

Shuttle 2: R 6 + 3—3—3—4. Continue until there are 4 motifs.

Star No. 5. One Shuttle

R 4—2—2—2—2—4. Jk 6 Hs. R 2 + 2 × 10—4. Jk 6 Hs.

  R 4 + 2 × 10—2. Jk 6 Hs. R 4 + 2—2—2—2—4.

  R 4 + 2—2—2—2—2—2 + 4.

Purpose: For mobile, table cloth or handkerchief insertions
Yarn: D.M.C. No. 30
Size: 6·5 cm. (2$\frac{5}{8}$ in.), 4·5 cm. (1$\frac{3}{4}$ in.), 5 cm. (2 in.), 2·5 cm. (1 in.), 2 cm. ($\frac{7}{8}$ in.)
Abbreviations: Number = number of double stitches between the picots;
  Ir = Inner ring, R = ring, C = chain, Jk = Josephine knot, Hs = half stitch,
  + = joining, 3 × 7 = 3 — 3 — 3 — 3 — 3 — 3 — 3, — = picot

Star No. 1. Two Shuttles
Shuttle 1: R 5 — 4 — 2 — 2 — 4 — 5. C 6.
Shuttle 2: R 4 — 3 — 3 — 3 — 3 — 3 — 5.
Shuttle 1: C 6. R 5 + 4 + 2 — 2 — 4 — 5. C 6.
Shuttle 2: R 4 — 3 + 3 — 3 — 4. R 4 + 3 × 8 — 4. R 4 + 3 — 3 — 3 — 4.
Shuttle 1: C 6.
Repeat 6 times.

Star No. 2. One Shuttle and Second Thread
R 5 — 5 — 5 — 5. C 10 — 10. Repeat 4 times. C 10 — 5 — 5.
  R 5 — 5 + 5 — 5. C 7 — 3 — 3 — 7. R 5 — 5 + 5 — 5. C 5 — 5 — 10.

Star No. 3. One Shuttle and Second Thread
Row 1: R 3 × 12. R 3 + 3 × 11. R 3 + 3 × 11. R 3 + 3 × 10 + 3.
Row 2: R 6 + 6. C 3 × 7.

Star No. 4. One Shuttle
R 6 — 6 (middle). R 3 — 3 — 2 — 2 — 4. Jk 6 Hs.
  R 2 + 4 — 2 — 2 — 2 — 4 — 2. Jk 6 Hs. R 4 + 2 — 2 — 3 — 3.
Repeat 4 times.

Star No. 5. One Shuttle
R 6 — 6. R 5 — 2 — 2 — 2 — 5. R 5 + 3 × 8 — 5. R 5 + 2 — 2 — 2 — 5.

Purpose: For mobile, table-cloth or handkerchief insertions

Yarn: D.M.C. No. 30

Size: 5·5 cm. ($2\frac{1}{4}$ in.), 4 cm. ($1\frac{5}{8}$ in.), 4·5 cm. ($1\frac{3}{4}$ in.), 3·5 cm. ($1\frac{3}{8}$ in.), 2·5 cm (1 in.)

Abbreviations: Number = number of double stitches between the picots, Ir = inner ring, R = ring, C = chain, Jk = Josephine knot, Hs = half stitch, + = joining, $3 \times 7 = 3 — 3 — 3 — 3 — 3 — 3 — 3$, — = picot

Star No. 1. One Shuttle and Second Thread

Row 1: R 3 — 2 — 2 — 3. R 5 — 3 — 2 — 2 — 2 — 2 — 3 — 5. Repeat 14 times and link as the illustration shows.

Row 2: + C 3 — 2 × 8 — 3 +. C 3 + 2 × 8 — 3 +. Repeat 14 times.

Star No. 2. One Shuttle and Second Thread

R 10 — 10. C 5 — 5 — 10. R 10 + 10. R 10 — 10. R 10 — 10.
  C 10 + 5 — 5. R 10 + 10. C 7 — 3 — 3 — 7. R 10 + 10.
  Repeat 4 times.

Star No. 3. One Shuttle and Second Thread

Row 1: R 5 — 5 — 5 — 5. Jk 8 Hs. Repeat 8 times and link as the illustration shows.

Row 2: R 6 + 6. C 3 × 7. Repeat 8 times.

Star No. 4. One Shuttle and Second Thread

Jk 8 Hs. R 5 — 2 — 2 — 2 — 2 — 5. R 5 + 3 — 2 — 2 — 2 — 2 — 3 — 5.
  R 5 + 2 — 2 — 2 — 2 — 5. Jk 8 Hs. R 6 — 6 (middle ring).
  C 5 + 2 — 2 — 2 — 2 — 5. R 6 + 6 (middle ring).

Star No. 5. One Shuttle and Second Thread

R 4 — 4. C 2 × 7. Repeat 5 times. Then work R 4 + 4.

Purpose: For mobile, table-cloth or handkerchief insertions
Yarn: D.M.C. No. 30
Size: 5 cm. (2 in.), 4 cm. ($1\frac{5}{8}$ in.), 3·5 cm. ($1\frac{3}{8}$ in.), 2 cm. ($\frac{7}{8}$ in.)
Abbreviations: Number = number of double stitches between the picots,
 Ir = inner ring, R = ring, C = chain, Jk = Josephine knot, Hs = half stitch,
 + = joining, $3 \times 6 = 3$—3—3—3—3—3, — = picot

Star No. 1. One Shuttle and Second Thread
Ir: 2×12. Tie threads together but do not cut.
Row 1: R12—5—5—12 +.   Repeat 12 times.
 Then work R 12 + 5—5—12 +.   Tie threads together and cut.
Row 2: R + 9 + 10.   C 10—10 +. R9 + 10.   C 10—10 +. Leave 0·5 cm
 thread before next R.   R 7—5—3—4.   R 4 + 8—8—4.
 R 4 + 3—5—7 (join to loop of thread twice, then to picot).   R 9 + 10.
 C 10 + 10 +.
Repeat 4 times.

Star No. 2. One Shuttle
Ir = 2×8.   Tie threads together but do not cut.
Row 1: R 8—4—4—8 +.   Repeat 8 times.   Then work R 8 + 4—4—8 +.
Row 2: R 2 + 2.   R 6—4—2—2—4—6.   Repeat 16 times.
Then work R 6 + 4—2—2—4—6.

Star No. 3. Two Shuttles
Shuttle 1: R 3×6.
Shuttle 2: R 3×10.
Shuttle 1: C 3 + 3 $\times$ 6.   R 3—3 + 3 + 3—3—3.
 R 3 + 3—3—3—3—3.   C 3 + 3 $\times$ 6.
Repeat 4 times.

Star No. 4. One Shuttle
R 6—6.   R 5—3—3—3—3—5.   Jk 8 Hs.   R 5 + 3—3—3—3—5.
Repeat 6 times.   Then work R 6 + 6.

Star No. 5. One Shuttle
R 5—3—2—2—2—2—3—5.   Repeat 4 times.
 Then work R 5 + 3—2—2—2—2—3—5.

Other Patterns for the Mobile

Purpose: For mobile, table-cloth or handkerchief insertions

Yarn: D.M.C. No. 30

Size: 6 cm. ($2\frac{3}{8}$ in.), 5 cm. (2 in.), 4·5 cm. ($1\frac{7}{8}$ in.), 4 cm. ($1\frac{5}{8}$ in.), 2 cm. ($\frac{7}{8}$ in.)

Abbreviations: Number = number of double stitches between the picots, Ir = inner ring, R = ring, C = chain, + = joining, $3 \times 6 = 3 — 3 — 3 — 3 — 3 — 3$, — = picot

Star No. 1. Two Shuttles

Ir = 5×5.   Tie together for fifth picot and cut.

Shuttle 1: R 5 — 5 — 5 — 5.   C 5 (shuttle 2: R 5 — 5 + (in Ir) 5 — 5) 5.
   R 5 + 5 — 5 — 5.   C 5 — 5.   Three-leaved clover: R 5 + 5 — 5 — 5.
   R 5 + 5 — 5 — 5.   R 5 + 5 — 5 — 5.   C 5 + 5.

Repeat 5 times.

Star No. 2. One Shuttle and Second Thread

Ir = 4×8.   Tie together for eighth picot and cut.
   R 2 — 2 — 2 — 2 + (in Ir) 2 — 2 — 2 — 2.   C 2 × 16.
   R 2 — 2 — 2 + 2 + 2 — 2 — 2 — 2.   C 2 + 2 + 2 × 14.

Repeat 4 times.

Star No. 3. Two Shuttles

Shuttle 1: R 10 — 10 — 3 — 4 — 4 — 6 — 6 — 4 — 4 — 3.   C 3 × 6.
   R 3 — 3 — 3 + 3 — 3 — 3.   C 3 × 6.   R 3 — 3 + 3 + 3 — 3 — 3.   C 3 × 6.
   R 3 — 3 + 3 + 3 — 3 — 3.   C 6 — 6 (shuttle 2: Three-leaved clover:
   R 6 + 3 × 6 — 6.   R 6 + 6 — 6 — 6.   R 6 + 3 × 6 — 6) 6 + 6.
   R 3 — 3 — 3 + 3 — 3 — 3.   C 3 × 6.   R 3 — 3 + 3 + 3 — 3 — 3.
   C 3 × 6.   R 3 — 3 + 3 + 3 — 3 — 3.   C 3 × 6.

Star No. 4. One Shuttle

Ir = 4×8.   Tie together for eighth picot but do not cut.
   R 8 — 3 × 10 — 8 +.   R 8 + 3 — 3 — 3 — 8 +.
Then work R 8 + 3 × 10 — 8 +.

Repeat alternately, 4 times.

Star No. 5. One Shuttle and Second Thread

R 5 — 5.   C 7 — 7.   R 5 + 5.   C 7 — 7.

The pattern consists of 5 rings and 5 chains.

Purpose: For mobile, table-cloth or handkerchief insertions
Yarn: D.M.C. No. 30
Size: 6·5 cm. (2⅝ in.), 5 cm. (2 in.), 4·5 cm. (1⅞ in.), 3·5 cm. (1⅜ in.), 3 cm. (1¼ in.)
Abbreviations: Number = number of double stitches between picots, Ir = inner
  ring, R = ring, C = chain, + = joining, 5 × 4 = 5 — 5 — 5 — 5, — = picot

Star No. 1. Two Shuttles
Shuttle 1: R3 × 8. R3 + 3 × 11. R3 + 3 × 7. C3 × 8 +. C3 + 3 × 7.
  R3 — 3 — 3 — 3 + 3 — 3 — 3 — 3. R3 + 3 — 3 — 3 — 3 — 3 — 3 — 3.
Shuttle 2: R3 + 3 × 11.
Shuttle 1: C3 + 3 × 7. C3 + 3 × 7.
Repeat 3 times.

Star No. 2. One Shuttle and Second Thread
R2 × 13. C2 × 11. R2 — 2 — 2 — 2 + 2 × 9. C2 × 11.
The pattern has 9 rings and 9 chains.

Star No. 3. One Shuttle and Second Thread
R5 — 5 — 5 — 5. R5 + 5 — 5 — 5. R5 + 5 — 5 — 5. C5 × 5.
  R5 — 5 + 5 — 5. C5 × 4. R5 — 5 + 5 — 5. C5 × 4.
  R5 — 5 + 5 — 5. C5 × 6. R5 — 5 + 5 — 5. C5 × 4.
  R5 — 5 + 5 — 5. C5 × 4. R5 — 5 + 5 — 5. C5 — 5 — 5 — 5 + 5.

Star No. 4. One Shuttle and Second Thread
Ir: 4 × 7.   Tie together for seventh picot and cut.
  R5 — 5 — 5 — 5. R5 + 5 — 5 — 5. C7 + 7 (+ in Ir).
  R5 + 5 — 5 — 5. R5 + 5 — 5 — 5. C7 + 7.
Repeat until the outer edge has 14 rings.

Star No. 5. One Shuttle and Second Thread
R4 — 4. C7 — 2 — 2 — 7 — 3. R6 — 2 — 2 — 2 — 6 + 6 — 2 — 2 — 6.
  R6 + 2 — 2 — 6 — 2 — 2 — 6 — 2 — 2 — 6.
  R6 + 2 — 2 — 6 — 6 — 2 — 2 — 6. C3 + 7 — 2 — 2 — 7. R4 + 4.

Purpose: For mobile, table-cloth or handkerchief insertions

Yarn: D.M.C. No. 30

Size: 7·5 cm. (3 in.), 6 cm. (2⅜ in.), 5 cm. (2 in.), 4·5 cm. (1⅞ in.), 2·5 cm. (1 in.)

Abbreviations: Number = number of double stitches between the picots, Ir = inner ring, R = ring, C = chain, + = joining, $3 \times 6 = 3 - 3 - 3 - 3 - 3 - 3$, — = picot

Star No. 1. Two Shuttles

Ir $= 3 \times 12$.　Tie together for twelfth picot and cut.

Shuttle 1: R 4 — 4 + (in middle ring) 4 — 4.　C 5.　R 3×6.　C 5.

Shuttle 2: R 4 + 4 + 4 — 4.　C 7 + 7 — 3.

Shuttle 1: R 3 + 3 — 3 — 3 — 3 — 3.　R 3 + 3×7.

　R 3 + 3 — 3 — 3 — 3 — 3.

Shuttle 2: C 3 + 7 — 7.　R 4 + 4 + 4 — 4.

Repeat 6 times.

Star No. 2. One Shuttle and Second Thread

R 6 — 6 (middle).　C 6.　R 6 — 6.　C 6 — 6 — 2 — 2 — 6.　R 6 + 6.

　C 6 — 2 — 2 — 2 — 2 — 6.　R 6 + 6.　C 6 — 2 — 2 — 6 — 6.　R 6 + 6.

　C 6.　R 6 + (in middle ring) 6.

Repeat 4 times.

Star No. 3. One Shuttle and Second Thread

R 4 — 4 — 10.　C — 10 — 10 (please note first picot).

　Leave 0·5 cm. thread before R 7 + 5 — 3 — 4.　R 4 + 8 — 8 — 4.

　R 4 + 3 — 5 — 7 (join to loop of thread twice, + in picot).

　R 4 — 4 — 10.　C 10 + 10.

Repeat 3 times.

Star No. 4. One Shuttle and Second Thread

R 5 — 3 — 3 — 3 — 5.　R 5 + 3 — 3 — 3 — 3 — 3 — 3 — 5.

　R 5 + 3 — 3 — 3 — 5.　C 15.　Link as shown in the illustration.

Repeat 5 times.

Star No. 5. One Shuttle and Second Thread

R 5×5.　C 2×11 +.　C 2 + 2×10 +.　C 2 + 2×10 +.

　C 2 + 2×10 +.　C 2 + $2 \times 9 + 2$.

49

Purpose: For mobile, table-cloth or handkerchief insertions
Yarn: D.M.C. No. 30
Size: 8 cm. ($3\frac{1}{4}$ in.), 4·5 cm. ($1\frac{7}{8}$ in.), 4 cm. ($1\frac{5}{8}$ in.), 3·5 cm. ($1\frac{3}{8}$ in.), 2·5 cm. (1 in.)
　Abbreviations: Number = number of double stitches between picots,
　R = ring, C = chain, + = joining, $3 \times 8 = 3 — 3 — 3 — 3 — 3 — 3 — 3 — 3$,
　— = picot

Star No. 1. Two Shuttles
Reverse work after each stage
Shuttle 1: R 5 — 5 — 5 — 5.
Shuttle 2: R 5 — 5 — 5 — 5.　C 10.　Three-leaved clover: R 5 + 5 — 5 — 5.
　R 5 + 5 — 5 — 5.　R 5 + 5 — 5 — 5.　C 10.　R 5 + 5 — 5 — 5.
Shuttle 1: R 5 + 5 — 5 — 5.　C 10.　R 5 + 5 — 5 — 5.
Shuttle 2: R 5 + 5 — 5 — 5.　C 10.　R 5 + 5 — 5 — 5.
Shuttle 1: R 5 + 5 — 5 — 5.　C 10.　R 5 + 5 — 5 — 5.
Shuttle 2: R 5 + 5 — 5 — 5.　C 10.
Now make a three-leaved clover at the top with shuttle 2 and the other side of
the pattern mirrored. Complete the work with
Shuttle 1: C 3 × 12.　Three-leaved clover: R 5 — 5 + 5 — 5.
　R 5 + 5 — 5 — 5.　R 5 + 5 + 5 — 5.　C 3 + 3 + 3 × 10.

Star No. 2. One Shuttle and Second Thread
R 5 — 3 — 3 — 3 — 5.　R 5 + 3 — 2 — 2 — 2 — 2 — 3 — 5.
　R 5 + 3 — 3 — 3 — 5.　C 3 × 11.　Link as shown in the illustration.
Repeat 5 times.

Star No. 3. Two Shuttles
Shuttle 1: R 3 × 10.　R 3 + 3 × 13.　R 3 + 3 × 9.　C 6 — 3 × 9.　R 4 + 4.
　C 3 × 8.　R 4 + 4.　C 3 — 3 — 3 — 3 — 3.　R 4 + 4.
Shuttle 2: R 6 — 6.
Shuttle 1: C 3 — 3 — 3 — 3 — 3.　R 4 + 4.　C 3 × 8.　R 4 + 4.
　C 3 × 9 + 6.

Star No. 4. One Shuttle and Second Thread
R 5 — 3 — 3 — 5.　C 7 — 2 — 7.　Link as shown in the illustration.
Repeat 7 times.

Star No. 5. One Shuttle and Second Thread
R 2 × 13.　C 2 × 8 +.　C 2 × 8.　R 2 — 2 — 2 + 2 — 2 — 2.　C 2 × 11.
　R 2 — 2 — 2 + 2 — 2 — 2.　C 2 × 8 +.　C 2 × 8 +.

5. Simple Patterns

Opposite. **Suggestion for joining stars. The edge consists of chains.**

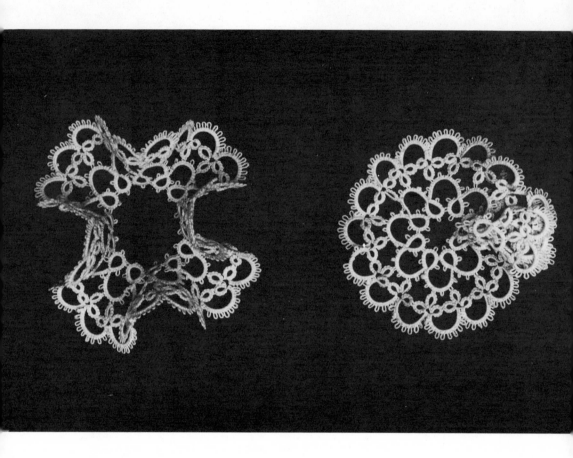

Frill

Purpose: Candlestick frill

Yarn: D.M.C. No. 30

Size: 7·5 cm. (3 in.)

Abbreviation: Number = number of double stitches between the picots,
   R = ring; C = chain, + = joining, — = picot

Number of shuttles: One, and second thread

Row 1: R 3 — 3 — 3 — 3 — 3 — 3.   C 3 — 3 — 3 — 3 — 3 — 3.
   R 3 — 3 + 3 — 3 — 3 — 3.   C 3 — 3 — 3 — 3 — 3 — 3.   Repeat 14 times.
Row 2: R 5 — 5.   R 5 + 5.   R 5 — 5.
   C 2 — 2 — 2 — 2 — 2 — 2 — 2 — 2 — 2 — 2 — 2.   Repeat 28 times.

Mat with Ring of Stars

See pattern for mobile on page 37. Thirteen stars were placed on a piece of fine linen and tacked to the two middle picots. Then the material was tucked in round the edges and closely buttonhole stitched, at the same time securing the stars, and finally cutting away surplus material.

Eye of the Sun

Yarn: D.M.C. No. 60

Size: 15 cm. ($5\frac{7}{8}$ in.)

Abbreviations: Number = number of double stitches between the picots, Ir = inner ring, R = ring, + = joining, — = picot

Number of shuttles: One

Ir = 2 —2 —2 —2 —2 —2 —2 —2 —2 —2 —2 —2. Tie ends and cut.
R 7 + 7. R 7 —2 —2 —2 —2 —2 —2 —7. Repeat 12 times.

The illustration shows a round piece of very fine linen with twelve stars sewn to it. The stars were placed on the linen and seamed to it by the inner rings. The material was cut close to the edges so that it follows the shape of the stars.

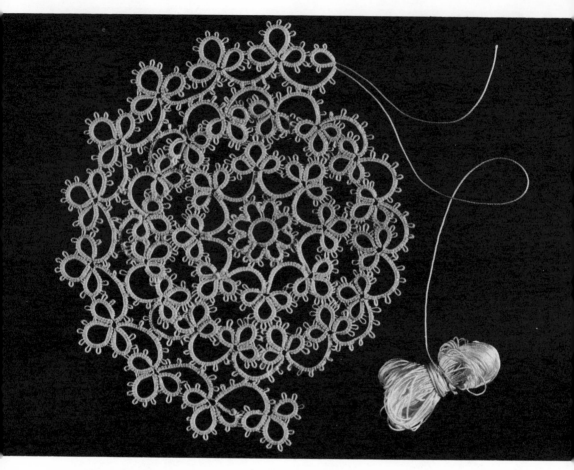

Flowery Meadow

Yarn: D.M.C. No. 30

Size: 13 cm. (5¼ in.)

Abbreviations: Number = number of double stitches between the picots, Ir = inner ring, R = ring, C = chain, + = joining, 2 × 5 = 2 — 2 — 2 — 2 — 2, — = picot

Number of shuttles: One, and second thread

Ir: 4 × 8. C 2 × 6 +. C 2 + 2 × 5 +. C 2 + 2 × 5 +. C 2 + 2 × 5 +. C 2 + 2 × 5 +. C 2 + 2 × 5 +. C 2 + 2 × 5 +. C 2 + 2 × 5 +.

Row 1: Three-leaved clover: R 5 — 2 — 2 — 2 — 2 — 5. R 5 + 2 — 2 — 2 — 2 — 2 — 2 — 5. R 5 + 2 — 2 — 2 — 2 — 5. C 3 — 8 + 8 — 3. Repeat 8 times.

Row 2: Three-leaved clover: R 5 — 2 — 2 — 2 — 2 — 5. R 5 + 2 — 2 — 2 — 2 — 2 — 2 — 5. C 4 × 7. Repeat 16 times.

Row 3: Three-leaved clover: R 6 — 3 — 3 — 3 — 3 — 6. R 6 + 3 — 3 — 3 — 3 — 3 — 3 — 6. R 6 + 3 — 3 — 3 — 3 — 6. C 4 — 4 — 4 + 4 — 4 — 4. Repeat 16 times.

Chrysanthemum

Yarn: D.M.C. No 30

Size: 13 cm. (5¼ in.)

Abbreviations: Number = number of double stitches between the picots, Ir = inner ring, R = ring, C = chain, + = joining, — = picot

Number of shuttles: One, and second thread

Ir: 8 — 3 — 3 — 8.   Repeat 10 times.   Link as shown in the illustration.

Row 1: Three-leaved clover: R 5 — 3 — 3 — 3 — 5.   R 5 + 5 — 3 — 3 — 5 — 5.
R 5 + 3 — 3 — 3 — 5.   C 5 — 10 + 10 — 5.

Row 2: Three-leaved clover: Same as row 1.   C 5 — 5.   R 5 + 5 — 5.
C 5 — 3 — 3 — 5.   R 5 + 5 — 5.   C 5 — 3 — 3 — 5.   R 5 + 5 — 5.
C 5 — 3 — 3 — 5.   R 5 + 5 — 5.   C 5 — 5.

Olden Times

Purpose: Window screen, runner, mats

Yarn: D.M.C. No. 30

Size: 36 × 40 cm. (14¼ × 15⅞ in.)

Abbreviations: Number = number of double stitches between the picots, Ir = inner ring, R = ring, C = chain, + = joining, 3 × 4 = 3 — 3 — 3 — 3, — = picot

Number of shuttles: One, and second thread

Ir: 3 × 8.   Tie together for eighth picot and cut.

Row 1: R 3 — 3 — 3 + (in middle ring) 3 — 3 — 3.   C 3 × 4.
R 3 — 3 + 3 + 3 — 3 — 3.   C 6 × 5 etc.   When the small stars are to be placed in among the larger stars, make the chain in the corners 6 — 6 — 3 + 3 — 6 — 6.

Row 2: R 3 — 3 — 3 + 3 — 3 — 3.   C 3 × 4.   R 3 — 3 + 3 + 3 — 3 — 3.
C 3 × 7.   R 3 — 3 — 3 + 3 — 3 — 3.   C 3 × 4.   R 3 — 3 + 3 + 3 — 3 — 3.
C 3 × 10 (corner).

The Grid   (Illustrated on page 62)

Yarn: D.M.C. No. 30

Size: 20 cm. (7⅞ in.)

Abbreviations: Number = number of knots between the picots, R = ring, C = chain, + = joining, — = picot

Number of shuttles: One, and second thread

Centre: R 7 — 3 — 7.   Repeat 4 times. Tie ends and cut.
R 3 — 3 — 3 + 3 — 3 — 3.   C 6 — 6 — 6 — 6 — 6 (corner).
R 3 — 3 + 3 + 3 — 3 — 3.   C 6 — 6.   Repeat round the inner four-leaved clover. Join the four stars as in the illustration.

The middle pattern

Row 1: R 5 — 5 — 5 — 5.   C 5 + 5.   Repeat all along the straight section.
Corner: C 5 + 7.   Three-leaved clover: R 5 + 5 — 5 — 5.
R 5 + 5 — 5 — 5 — 5.   R 5 + 5 — 5 — 5.   C 7 + 5.

Row 2: Work straight section as row 1.   Corner: R 5 — 5 + 3 — 3 — 3.
C 5 — 5 — 5 — 5 — 5.   R 3 — 3 — 3 + 5 — 5.   C 5 — 5.
R 5 + 5 + 5 — 5 etc.

The edge is made up of the same stars as the centre. The illustration overleaf shows how they are put together.

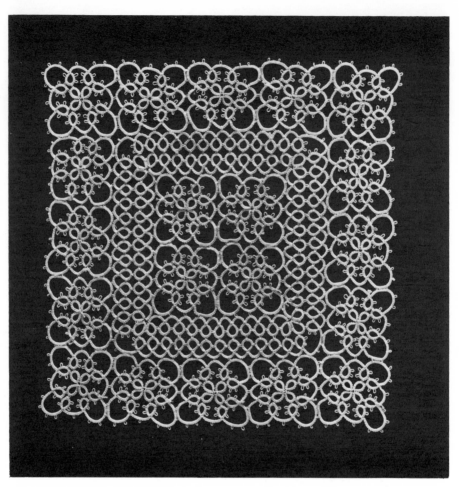

The Grid. Pattern on page 61.

Arabesque

Purpose: Mat for cup and saucer, small runner for cream and sugar

Yarn: D.M.C. No. 70

Size: 7 cm. ($2\frac{7}{8}$ in.), 14 cm. ($5\frac{1}{2}$ in.)

Abbreviations: Number = number of double stitches between the picots,
  Ir = inner ring, R = ring, C = chain, $2 \times 6 = 2—2—2—2—2—2$,
  — = picot

Number of shuttles: One, and second thread

Ir: 2×6.   C 4×4.   Repeat 4 times and link as in the illustration.

Row 1: R 2×6.   C 4×4.   Repeat 12 times.

Row 2: Same as row 1.

Row 3: R 2×6.   C 4×4.   Repeat 24 times.

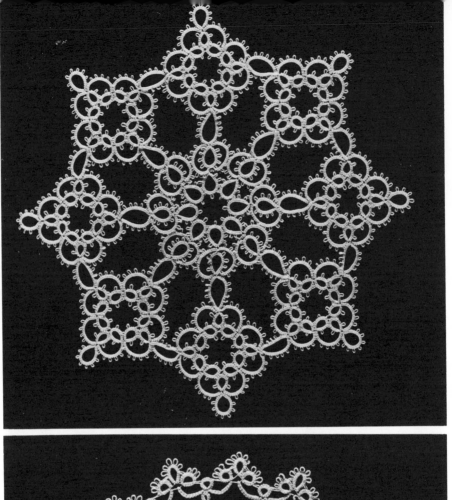

Ice Crystal

Yarn: D.M.C. No. 30

Size: 17 cm ($6\frac{7}{8}$ in.)

Abbreviations: Number = number of double stitches between the picots, R = ring, C = chain, + = joining, $3 \times 5 = 3 - 3 - 3 - 3 - 3$, — = picot

Number of shuttles: Two

Shuttle 1: R3 × 6. C3 × 7. R3 — 3 + 3 + 3 — 3 — 3. R3 + 3 × 5.
   C3 + 3 × 6. R3 — 3 + 3 + 3 — 3 — 3. C3 + 3 × 6 (towards middle).
   R3 × 10. C3 + 3 × 8 +.

Shuttle 2: R3 × 10 (middle ring).

Shuttle 1: C3 × 9 +. C3 + 3 × 6 +. C3 + 3 × 6.
   R3 — 3 + 3 + 3 — 3 — 3. R3 + 3 × 5. C3 + 3 × 6.
   R3 — 3 + 3 + 3 — 3 — 3. C3 + 3 × 5.

Repeat 8 times.
   C3 × 7 +. C3 + 3 × 6. R3 — 3 + 3 + 3 — 3 — 3.
   R3 + 3 — 3 — 3 — 3 — 3. C3 + 3 × 6. R3 — 3 + 3 + 3 — 3 — 3.

Shuttle 2: R3 + 3 × 9.

Shuttle 1: C3 + 3 × 6. R3 — 3 + 3 + 3 — 3 — 3.
   R3 + 3 — 3 + 3 + 3 — 3. C3 + 3 × 6.

Snow Star

Yarn: D.M.C. No. 80

Size: 12 cm. ($4\frac{7}{8}$ in.)

Abbreviations: Number = number of double stitches between the picots, Ir = inner ring, R = ring, C = chain, $2 \times 12 = 2 - 2 - 2 - 2 - 2 - 2 - 2 - 2 - 2 - 2 - 2$, — = picot

Number of shuttles: One, and second thread

Ir: 2 × 12.   Tie ends for twelfth picot.

Row 1: R5 + 5. R5 — 5 — 5 — 5.   Repeat 12 times.

Row 2: R5 — 5. C10 + 10.   Repeat 12 times.

Row 3: R5 — 5 — 5 — 5. C3 + 3. R5 — 5 — 5 — 5. C6.
   R5 — 5 — 5 — 5. C6. R5 — 5 — 5 — 5. C3 + 3.

Row 4: R5 — 5. C10 + 10.

Row 5: R5 — 5 — 5 +. C + 10.
   Three-leaved clover: R5 + 2 — 2 — 2 — 2 — 5.
   R5 + 2 — 2 — 2 — 2 — 2 — 5. R5 + 2 — 2 — 2 — 5. C10 +.

Coppelia

Yarn: D.M.C. No. 30

Size: 13 cm. (5¼ in.)

Abbreviations: Number = number of double stitches between the picots,
   R = ring, C = chain, + = joining, — = picot

Number of shuttles: One, and second thread

Row 1: R 6 — 6 — 6 — 6 — 6 — 6.   C 6 — 6 — 6 — 6 — 6 — 6.
   R 6 — 6 + 6 — 6 — 6 — 6.   Repeat 7 times.

Row 2: R 6 — 6 — 6 + 6 — 6 — 6.   C 6 — 6 — 6 — 6 — 6 — 6.
   Repeat 14 times.

Row 3: R 5 + 5.   R 10 — 10.   C 5 — 10 — 5 +.   R 5 + 5.
   R 10 — 10.   C 5 — 10 — 5 +.   In order to end row 4 evenly, make three
   pattern sections instead of the two which occur in each chain in row 2. The
   last row must be divisible by three.

Row 4: R 4 — 4 + 4 — 4.   R 5 — 5.   R 4 + 4 + 4 — 4.
   R 6 + 3 — 3 — 3 — 3 — 3 — 3 — 6.   R 4 + 4 + 4 — 4.   R 5 + 5.

Heptagon

Yarn: D.M.C. No. 30

Size: 11·5 cm. ($4\frac{5}{8}$ in.)

Abbreviations: Number = number of double stitches between the picots,
R = ring, C = chain, + = joining, — = picot

Number of shuttles: One, and second thread

R 4 — 4 — 4 — 4 — 4 — 4.   C 4 — 4 — 4 — 4 — 4 — 4.
  R 4 — 4 + 4 — 4 — 4 — 4.

Repeat 7 times.

The illustration shows the joining.

The octagon is made like the heptagon but with eight rings and chains.

Size and shape can be varied according to taste.

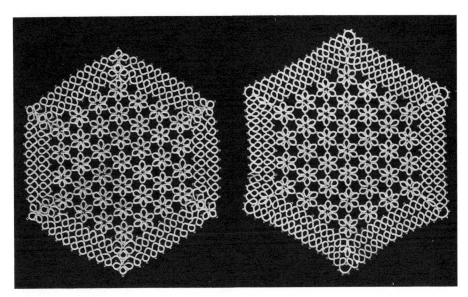

Hexagonal Mats

These mats are variations on the centre piece of the Star pattern below. They can be joined together into a tea-table-cloth.

The Star

Yarn: D.M.C. No. 30

Size: 39 cm. (15$\frac{3}{8}$ in.)

Abbreviations: Number = number of double stitches between the picots, R = ring, C = chain, + = joining, — = picot

Number of shuttles: One, and second thread

The centre motif: R 5 — 5 — 5 — 5. R 5 + 5 — 5 — 5. R 5 + 5 — 5 — 5.
   R 5 + 5 — 5 — 5. R 5 + 5 — 5 — 5 —. R 5 + 5 — 5 + 5.

Tie threads and cut. Join small sections as illustrated.

The motif surrounding the centre consists of alternately, R 5 — 5 — 5 — 5 and C 5 — 5.

The star points are each made up of seven stars. They are worked as follows: R 5 — 5 — 5 — 5 and C 5 — 5 — 5 — 5.

Tendril

Purpose: Collar

Yarn: D.M.C. No. 30

Size: 5 cm. (2 in.) wide

Abbreviations: Number = number of double stitches between the picots, R = ring, C = chain, + = joining, — = picot

Number of shuttles: One, and second thread

Row 1: R 5 — 5 — 5 — 5.   C 5 — 3 — 3 — 3 — 5.   Repeat until the work is the required length.

Row 2: R 5 — 5 — 5 — 5.   C 7 + 3 + 3 + 3 + 7 (opposite C in row 1).

Row 3: R 5 — 5 + 5 — 5.   C 10 — 5 — 5. R 5 — 5 + 5 — 5.
  R 5 — 5 + 5 — 5.   C 5 + 5 — 10.   R 5 — 5 + 5 — 5.

Row 4: R 5 + 5 + 5.   C 10 — 2 — 2 — 2 — 2 — 10.

The Big Cross

Purpose: Bookmark for bible or prayer book

Yarn: D.M.C. No. 30

Size: 11 cm. (4⅜ in.) cord

Abbreviations: Number = number of double stitches between the picots, R = ring, C = chain, + = joining, — = picot

Number of shuttles: One, and second thread

Begin with the three-leaved clover at the inner edge of the right horizontal section.

Three-leaved clover: R 5 — 5 — 5 — 5. R 5 + 5 — 5 — 5 (the middle picot needs to be quite long). R 5 + 5 — 5 — 5. C 5 — 5. R 5 + 5 — 5 — 5. C 5 — 5. R 5 + 5 — 5 — 5. C 5 — 5 — 5 — 5. R 5 — 5 + 5 — 5. C 5 — 5 — 5 — 5. R 5 — 5 + 5 — 5. C 5 — 5. R 5 + 5 + 5 — 5. C 5 — 5.

Make another three-leaved clover and work towards the top of the upright.

The flower at the top: Three-leaved clover: R 5 — 5 — 5 — 5.

R 5 + 5 — 5 — 5. R 5 + 5 — 5 — 5. C 25 — 5 (should not be tautly pressed together). R 5 — 5 + (the tip of the cross) — 5.

The second flower as well as the other half of the cross are mirror-worked.

71

The Small Cross

Purpose: Bookmark for bible or prayer book

Yarn: D.M.C. No. 40

Size: 7·5 cm. (3 in.) without cord

Abbreviations: Number = number of double stitches between the picots, R = ring, C = chain, 2 × 7 = 2 — 2 — 2 — 2 — 2 — 2 — 2, — = picot

Number of shuttles: One, and second thread

All rings: 4 — 4.

All chains: 2 × 7 (except the chain at the top which has 2 × 8, i.e. 7 picots). Begin in the corner between horizontal and upright bars: R 3. C. R attach to preceding chain. R. C. R attach to preceding chain. R. C etc. as illustrated. The edges of the horizontal bars are made with R. C. R. C. and both these rings are attached respectively to the preceding rings. This constitutes the turn towards the middle and the completion of the patterns. Make three rings close together where the horizontal and upright bars meet at the lower edge. Secure them to the corresponding rings. (The third is free.)

Instead of with cords the work can be finished off with: R. C. R. C. R. C. R. C. (The chains 2 × 6) C 30. R 4 + 4. (Attach to the picot at the tip of the cross) C 30.

Finish off with R. C. R. C. R. C. R. C.

6. Advanced Patterns

74

The Crown

Yarn: D.M.C. No. 30

Size: 21·5 cm. (8½ in.)

Abbreviations: Number = number of double stitches between the picots, R = ring, C = chain, + = joining, 4 × 12 = 4—4—4—4—4—4—4—4—4—4—4—4, — = picot

Number of shuttles: Two

Row 1: Shuttle 1: R 3—3—3—3—6—6.
    C 7 + (shuttle 2: R 4—4—4—4) 7. R 6 + 6—6—6.
    C 7 + (shuttle 2: R 4 + 4—4—4) 7.
    R 6 + 6—3—3—3—3. C 7 (shuttle 2: R 4 + 4—4—4).
    All R in brackets make up the inner line.
    Shuttle 2: C 3—3—3—3—3. R 4 + 4—4—4.
    Shuttle 1: C 7. R 3—3—3—3—6—6. Continue until the required length and finish off with C 3—3—3—3—3.

Row 2: Use shuttle and second thread. R 3—3—3—3 + 7—7 (join to the first ring in the group of three rings). C 7—7. R 7 + 7 + 7—7. (Join to second ring in the group of three rings). C 7—7.
    R 7 + 7 + 3—3—3—3 (join to third ring in the group of three rings).
    C 3—3—3—3—3—3—3—3. Finish the row.

Finishing edge: R 4 × 12. Tie together threads for twelfth picot and cut.
    R 3—3—3 + 4—4 (join to twelfth picot in the ring and tuck in the cut ends).
    C 3—3 + 3—3—3—3—3—3 (join to C to the left of the long C).
    R 4 + 4 + 4—4. C 3—3—3—3—3—3. R 4 + 4 + 4—4.
    C 3—3—3—3—3. R 4—4 + 4—4.
    C 3—3—3—3—3—3—3—3. R 4 + 4 + 4—4.
    C 3—3—3—3—3. R 4—4 + 4—4. C 3—3—3—3—3.
    R 4 + 4 + 4—4. C 3—3—3—3—3 + 3—3 (join to C to the right of the long C). R 4 + 4 + 3—3—3. Join threads and cut.

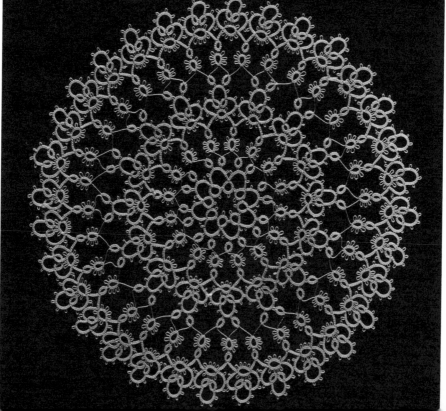

Sunflower

Yarn: D.M.C. No. 30

Size: 15 cm. ($5\frac{7}{8}$ in.)

Abbreviations: Number = number of double stitches between the picots, Ir = inner ring, R = ring, C = chain, + = joining, $3 \times 6 = 3 — 3 — 3 — 3 — 3 — 3$, — = picot.

Number of shuttles: Two

Centre: R 3×10. R $3 + 3 \times 9$. R $3 + 3 \times 9$. R $3 + 3 \times 8 + 3$.

Row 1: Shuttle 1: R 3×6 (ring No. 1).

Shuttle 2: C $3 + 3 \times 8$.

Shuttle 1: R $3 + 3 \times 5$ (ring No. 2).

C 3×8. R 3×6. C $3 — 3 — 3 +$ (in centre) $3 — 3 — 3 +$ (in previous ring). C $3 \times 8 +$ (in the bottom of ring No. 2).

Shuttle 2: C $3 + 3 \times 8$. Repeat from shuttle 1 immediately above. Every third pattern is joined to the centre. The long C are joined opposite each other in the three centre picots. See illustration.

Row 2: Shuttle 1: R 3×8. C $2 — 3 \times 8 +$ (in previous R).

Shuttle 2: C $3 — 3 — 3 + 3 + 3 — 3 — 3$ (joining in the C of the first row).

Shuttle 1: R 3×8. C $3 — 3 — 3 + 3 + 3 — 3 — 3 — 3 — 2 +$. R 3×8. C $2 + 3 \times 8 — 2 +$. R 3×8. C $2 + 3 \times 8 +$.

Shuttle 2: C $3 — 3 — 3 + 3 + 3 — 3 — 3$.

Shuttle 1: R 3×8.

The Miracle

Yarn: D.M.C. No. 30

Size: 20 cm. ($7\frac{7}{8}$ in.)

Abbreviations: Number = number of double stitches between the picots, Ir = inner ring, R = ring, C = chain, + = joining, $4 \times 4 = 4 — 4 — 4 — 4$, — = picot

Number of shuttles: One, and second thread

Ir: $5 — 4 — 4 — 5$. C 4×5. Repeat 8 times and join as illustrated.

Row 1: R $6 + 6$. R 2×8.

Row 2: R $6 + 6$. C 6. R 2×8. C 4×4. R $6 + 6$. C 4×5. R $6 + 6$. C $4 \times 4 +$. C 6. R $6 + 6$.

Row 3: As row 1.

Row 4: R $6 + 6$. C 6. R 2×10. C 4×4. R $6 + 6$. C 4×5. R $6 + 6$. C $4 \times 4 +$. C 6. R $6 + 6$.

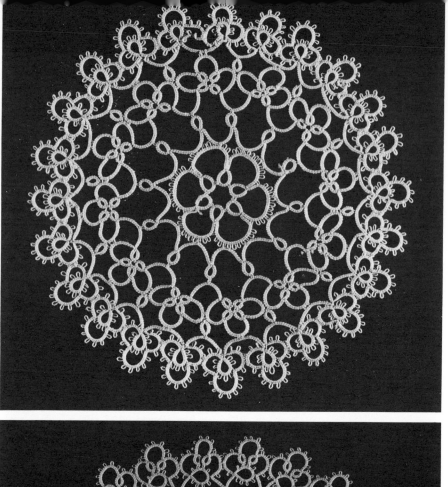

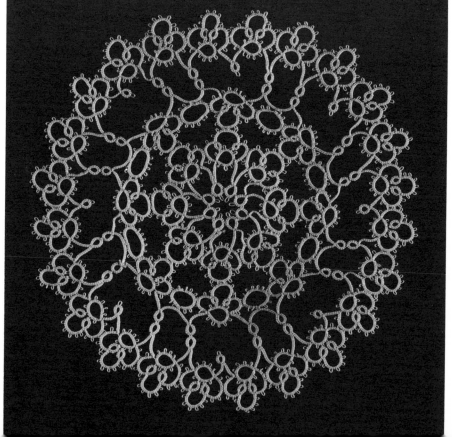

Mignonette

Yarn: D.M.C. No. 30

Size: 15 cm. ($5\frac{7}{8}$ in.)

Abbreviations: Number = number of double stitches between the picots, R = ring, C = chain, + = joining, $3 \times 6 = 3 - 3 - 3 - 3 - 3 - 3$.
— = picot

Number of shuttles: Two

Row 1: R 7 — 5 — 7.   C 5 — 2 × 12 — 5.   Repeat 6 times.
Row 2: R 8 — 8.   C 10 + 10.   Repeat 12 times and join as shown in illustration.
Row 3: Shuttle 1: R 5 — 5.
   Shuttle 2: C 10 + 10 (in previous row).
   Shuttle 1: R 5 — 5.   C 9 — 2 — 9.   R 5 + 5.   C 9 — 2 — 9.
   R 5 + 5.   C 9 — 2 — 9.   R 5 + 5.
   Shuttle 2: C 10 + 10.
   Shuttle 1: R 5 — 5.
Row 4: Shuttle 1: R 2 × 10.   C 3 × 6 +.   C 3 × 8 +.   C 3 × 6 +.
   Shuttle 2: C 10 + 2 + 10 (in previous row).
   Shuttle 1: R 2 × 10.   C 3 — 3 — 3 + 3 + 3 — 3 +.   C 3 × 8 +.
   C 3 × 6 +.
   Shuttle 2: C 11 (shuttle 1: R 7 + 7) 11.

Peony

Yarn: D.M.C. No. 30

Size: 19 cm. ($7\frac{1}{2}$ in.)

Abbreviations: Number = number of double stitches between the picots, R = ring, C = chain, + = joining, $3 \times 5 = 3 - 3 - 3 - 3 - 3$, — = picot

Number of shuttles: Two

Row 1: R 5 — 4 — 4 — 5.   C 10.   R 3 × 10.   C 3 × 5.   R 4 + 4.   C 3 × 7.
   R 4 + 4.   C 3 × 5 +.   C 10.   R 5 + 4 — 4 — 5 (middle).
Row 2: Shuttle 1: R 6 — 6.   C 10.   R 3 × 11.   C 3 × 5.   R 4 + 4.
   C 3 — 3 — 3 + 3 + 3 — 3 — 3.   R 4 + 4.   C 3 × 5 +.   C 10.   R 6 — 6.
   C 8 (shuttle 2: R 3 — 3 — 3 + 3 + 3 — 3 — 3 — 3 — 3 — 3 — 3 — 3 — 3.)
   8.   R 6 — 6.
Row 3: R 6 + 6.   C 10.   R 3 × 10.   C 3 × 6.   R 6 + 6.   C 3 × 7.
   R 6 + 6.   C 3 × 6 +.   C 7.   R 6 × 6.   C 7.

Lucky Clover

Yarn: D.M.C. No. 30

Size: 22 cm. ($8\frac{3}{4}$ in.)

Abbreviations: Number = number of double stitches between the picots, Ir = inner ring, R = ring, C = chain, $10 \times 5 = 10 - 10 - 10 - 10 - 10$, — = picot

Number of shuttles: One, and second thread

Row 1: R 15 — 10 — 5.   C 5.   Three-leaved clover: R 5 + 10 — 5.
R 5 + 7 — 7 — 5.   R 5 + 10 — 5.   C 5.   R 5 + 10 — 15.
C 5 — 10 × 5 — 5.   Repeat 8 times.

Row 2: Three-leaved clover: R 15 — 5.   R 5 + 5 — 5 — 5.   R 5 + 5 — 10.
C 10 — 5.   R 5 + 15 — 5.   C 5.   Three-leaved clover: R 5 + 10 — 5.
R 5 + 7 + 7 — 5.   R 5 + 10 — 5.   C 5.   R 5 + 15 — 5.
C 5 + 10.   R 10 + 5 — 5.   R 5 + 5 — 5 — 5.   R 5 + 15.
C 10 — 10 — 5 — 10 — 5 +.   C 5 + 10 — 5 — 10 — 10.   R 15 — 5.
R 5 + 5 + 5 — 5.   R 5 + 5 — 10.   C 10 — 5.   R 5 + 10 — 5.
R 5 + 10 — 5.   R 5 + 10 — 5.   C 5 + 10.   R 10 + 5 — 5.
R 5 + 5 — 5 — 5.   R 5 + 15.   C 10 + 10 — 5 — 10 — 5 +.
C 5 + 10 — 5 — 10 — 10.

Row 3: R 5 — 15 — 5.   C 5 — 10 + 5 + 10 — 10.   R 15 — 5.
R 5 + 5 + 5 — 5.   R 5 + 5 — 10.   C 10 — 5.   R 5 + 15 — 5.   C 5.
R 5 + 10 — 5.   R 5 + 15 — 5.   R 5 + 10 — 5.   C 5.   R 5 + 15 — 5.
C 5 + 10.   R 10 + 5 — 5.   R 5 + 5 — 5 — 5.   R 5 + 15.
C 10 + 10 + 5 + 10 — 5.

Water Lily

Yarn: D.M.C. No. 40

Size: 21·5 cm. (8½ in.)

Abbreviations: Number = number of double stitches between the picots, R = ring, C = chain, + = joining, 3 × 4 = 3 — 3 — 3 — 3, — = picot

Number of shuttles: Two

Row 1: Shuttle 1: R 3 × 8. R 3 × 8. C 3 × 6. R 3 × 9. R 3 × 9.
C 3 × 4.
Shuttle 2: R 3 × 8 (middle section). Make the fourth picot long enough for the other three rings to be joined to it.
Shuttle 1: C 3 × 4 +. C 3 + 3 × 5. Repeat 4 times.

Row 2: Shuttle 2: R 3 × 8.
Shuttle 1: C 3 + 3 × 11.
Shuttle 2: R 3 × 8.

Row 3: C 10 — 10 +.

Row 4: Shuttle 1: C 15 (shuttle 2: R 3 × 12.) 15 +.

Row 5: Shuttle 1: R 3 × 10. R 3 × 10.
Shuttle 2: R 3 × 12. R 3 × 12.
Shuttle 1: C 15 + 15.

Row 6: Shuttle 1: C 8 (shuttle 2: R 5 — 5.) 8 +. C 15 (shuttle 2: R 3 × 12.)
15 +.

Row 7: R 3 — 3 — 3 + 3 + 3 — 3 — 3 — 3. R 3 + 3 — 3 — 3 — 3 — 3 — 3 — 3.
C 15 — 10 +. C 10 + 15. R 3 — 3 — 3 + 3 + 3 — 3 — 3 — 3.
R 3 + 3 — 3 — 3 — 3 — 3 — 3 — 3. C 3 × 13.
R 3 — 3 — 3 — 3 + 3 — 3 — 3 — 3. R 3 + 3 — 3 — 3 — 3 — 3 — 3 — 3.
C 3 × 15. R 3 — 3 — 3 — 3 + 3 + 3 — 3 — 3.
R 3 + 3 — 3 — 3 — 3 — 3 — 3 — 3. C 3 × 13.
R 3 — 3 — 3 — 3 + 3 — 3 — 3 — 3. R 3 + 3 — 3 + 3 + 3 + 3 — 3 — 3.
Continue from the first C in the row.

Cascade

Yarn: D.M.C. No. 30

Size: 18·5 cm. (7½ in.)

Abbreviations: Number = number of double stitches between the picots, R = ring, C = chain, + = joining, 3 × 6 = 3 — 3 — 3 — 3 — 3 — 3, — = picot

Number of shuttles: Two

Shuttle 1: R 3 × 10.

Shuttle 2: R 3 × 12.   C 3 + 3 + 3 + 3 × 8.   C 3 × 7.   C 3 × 6.
    C 3 × 6 +.   C 3 × 7 +.   C 3 × 11 +.

Shuttle 1: R 3 + 3 + 3 + 3 × 7.   C 5 — 15.   R 3 × 8.   C 3 × 8 +.   R 3 × 8.
    C 3 + 3 × 7 +.   R 3 + 3 × 7.   C 3 + 3 × 7 +.   R 3 + 3 × 7.
    C 3 + 3 × 7 +.   R 3 × 8.   C 3 + 3 × 7 +.   C 15 + 5.   R 3 × 10.

Shuttle 2: R 3 × 12.   C 3 + 3 + 3 + 3 — 3 — 3 + 3 + 3 — 3 — 3 — 3 +.
    C 3 — 3 — 3 — 3 — 3 + 3 + 3.   R 3 × 6.   C 3 + 3 — 3 (shuttle 1:
    R 3 × 12.)   3 — 3 — 3 +.   Make the ring in brackets every third time. Make the fifth picot long enough for the other three middle rings to be joined to it.

Ace of Hearts

Yarn: D.M.C. No. 30

Size: 18 cm. ($7\frac{1}{8}$ in.)

Abbreviations: Number = number of double stitches between the picots, R = ring, C = chain, + = joining, $3 \times 6 = 3 - 3 - 3 - 3 - 3 - 3$, — = picot

Number of shuttles: Two

Shuttle 1: R 6 — 6 — 6 — 6.

Shuttle 2: R 6 — 6 — 6 — 6.   C 10.   R 6 + 6 — 6 — 6.   R 6 + 6 — 6 — 6.
R 6 + 6 — 6 — 6.   C 10.   R 6 + 6 — 6 — 6.

Shuttle 1: R 6 + 6 — 6 — 6.   C 10.   R 6 + 6 — 6 — 6.

Shuttle 2: R 6 + 6 — 6 — 6.   C 10.   R 6 + 6 — 6 — 6.

Shuttle 1: R 6 + 6 — 6 — 6.   C 10.   R 6 + 6 — 6 — 6.

Shuttle 2: R 6 + 6 — 6 — 6.   C 10.

Shuttle 1: R 6 + 10 — 10 — 6.   R 6 + 10 — 10 — 6.   R 6 + 10 — 10 — 6.

Shuttle 2: C 10.   R 6 + 6 + 6 — 6.

Shuttle 1: R 6 + 6 — 6 — 6.   C 10.   R 6 + 6 — 6 — 6.

Shuttle 2: R 6 + 6 — 6 — 6.   C 10.   R 6 + 6 — 6 — 6.

Shuttle 1: R 6 + 6 — 6 — 6.   C 10.   R 6 + 6 — 6 — 6.

Shuttle 2: R 6 + 6 — 6 — 6.   C 10.   R 6 + 6 — 6 — 6.   R 6 + 6 — 6 — 6.
R 6 + 6 — 6 — 6.   C 10.   R 6 + 6 — 6 — 6.

Shuttle 1: R 6 + 6 — 6 — 6.

Shuttle 2: C 6 + 3 — 3 +.   C 3 × 9.   R 6 — 6 + 6 — 6.   R 6 + 6 + 6 — 6.

Shuttle 1: R 6 — 6 — 6 — 6.

Shuttle 2: C 3 × 8.   R 6 — 6 + 6 — 6.   R 6 + 6 + 6 — 6.

Shuttle 1: R 6 — 6 — 6 — 6.

Shuttle 2: C 3 × 8.   R 6 — 6 + 6 — 6.   R 6 + 6 — 6 — 6.   R 6 + 6 + 6 — 6.
C 3 + 3 + 3 × 6.   R 6 — 6 + 6 — 6.   R 6 + 6 + 6 — 6.

Shuttle 1: R 6 — 6 — 6 — 6.

Shuttle 2: C 3 × 8.   R 6 — 6 + 6 + 6.   R 6 + 6 + 6 — 6.

Shuttle 1: R 6 — 6 — 6 — 6.

Shuttle 2: C 3 × 9 +.   C 3 — 3 (reverse work).

Shuttle 1: C 3 — 3 — 3 — 3 +.   C 3 × 8.   R 6 — 6 + 6 — 6.   C 3 × 6 +.
C 3 × 6.   R 6 — 6 + 6 — 6.   C 3 × 6.   R 6 — 6 + 6 — 6.   C 3 × 6.
R 6 — 6 + 6 — 6.   R 6 + 6 + 6 — 6.   C 3 × 6.   R 6 — 6 + 6 — 6.
C 3 × 6.   R 6 — 6 + 6 — 6.   C 3 × 6 +.   C 3 × 6.   R 6 — 6 + 6 — 6.
C 3 × 8 +.   C 3 — 3.

Repeat 4 times.

7.Crowns

3 patterns (pages 89-94)

Opposite: Faith. *For the pattern see page 90.*

Faith

Yarn: D.M.C. No. 20

Size: Height 5·5 cm. (2¼ in.) circumference 26 cm. (10¼ in.)

Abbreviations: Number = number of double stitches between the picots, R = ring, C = chain, + = joining, + — = joining and picot, 3 × 3 = 3 — 3 — 3, — = picot

Number of shuttles: Two

Row 1: Shuttle 1: R 3 × 10.   Shuttle 2: C 3 × 3.   Shuttle 1: R 3 — 3 + 3 + 3 — 3 — 3 — 3 — 3 — 3 — 3.   Shuttle 2: C 3 × 3.

Repeat until there are 33 rings and 33 chains.

Row 2: C 3 × 3 + — between each ring.

Row 3: Shuttle 1: R 3 × 11.   Shuttle 2: R 3 × 12.   C 3 + 3 + 3 × 10. Shuttle 1: R 3 + 3 × 7.   Shuttle 2: C 3 + 3 × 11 + .   Shuttle 1: R 3 + 3 + 3 × 9.   C 3 — 3 — 3 — 9 + 3 + 3 + 3 + 3 + 9 — 3 — 3 — 3.

Repeat until there are 11 pattern sections.

Charity

Yarn: D.M.C. No. 20

Size: Height 10 cm. (3⅞ in.) circumference 20 cm. (7⅞ in.)

Abbreviations: Number = number of double stitches between the picots, R = ring, C = chain, + = joining, — = picot

Number of shuttles: One, and second thread

Begin with the pattern at the bottom of the crown.

Row 1: Three-leaved clover: R 15 — 5.   R 5 + 5 — 5 — 5.   R 5 + 5 — 10. C 10 — 5.   R 5 + 15 — 5.   C 5.   Three-leaved clover: R 5 + 10 — 5. R 5 + 7 — 1 — 7 — 5.   R 5 + 10 — 5.   C 5.   R 5 + 15 — 5.   C 5 + 10. Three-leaved clover: R 10 + 5 — 5.   R 5 + 5 — 5 — 5.   R 5 + 15. C + 10 — 10 — 5 — 10 — 5 + .   C 5 + 10 — 5 — 10 — 10.

Repeat 7 times.

Row 2: R 5 — 15 — 5.   C 5 — 10 + 5 + 10 — 10.
Three-leaved clover: R 15 — 5.   R 5 + 5 + 5 — 5.   R 5 + 5 — 10. C 10 — 5.   R 5 + 15 — 5.   C 5.
Three-leaved clover at the top: R 5 + 10 — 5.   R 5 + 8 — 8 — 5. R 5 + 10 — 5.   C 5.   R 5 + 15 — 5.   C 5 + 10.
Three-leaved clover: R 10 + 5 — 5.   R 5 + 5 — 5 — 5.   R 5 + 15. C 10 + 10 + 5 + 10 — 5.

Row 3: R 5 — 5 — 5 — 5.   C 5.   R 5 + 5 — 5 — 5. C 2 + 1 + 2 (fasten every fifth chain to the bottom edge).

Row 4: C 5 (between each ring at the bottom).

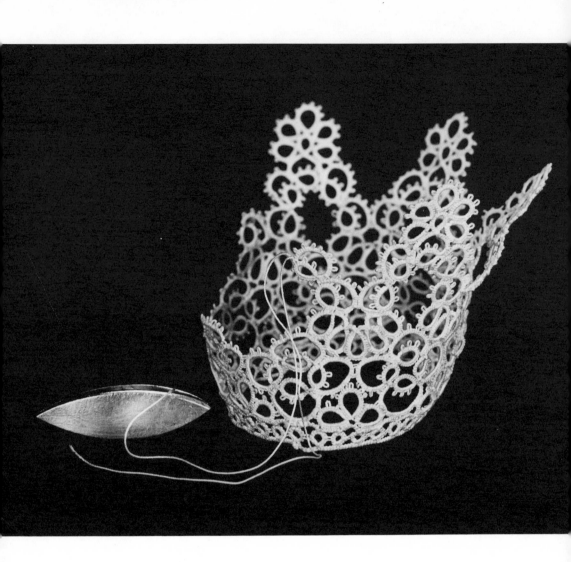

Pinnacles

Yarn: D.M.C. No. 20

Size: Height 9·5 cm. ($3\frac{7}{8}$ in.) circumference 22 cm. ($8\frac{7}{8}$ in.)

Abbreviations: Number = number of double stitches between the picots, R = ring, C = chain, + = joining, + — = joining and picot, 3 × 8 = 3 — 3 — 3 — 3 — 3 — 3 — 3 — 3, — = picot

Number of shuttles: Two

Row 1: Shuttle 1: R 3 — 3 — 3 — 3.
  Shuttle 2: C 6. (bottom edge). Make the ring and the chain alternately 35 times. Tie and secure the threads.

Row 2: Shuttle 1: R 3 — 3 — 3 — 3 — 3 — 3 — 3 — 6.
  R 6 + 3 — 3 — 3 — 3 — 3 — 3 — 6. R 6 + 3 — 3 — 3 — 3 — 3 — 3 — 3.
  Shuttle 2: C 3 + 3 + 3 + 3 — 3 + — 3 — 3 + — 3 — 3 + — 3.

Row 3: R 12 — 3 — 3 — 3 — 3. C — 3 × 10 + R 9 — 3 — 3 — 3.
  C 3 + 3 — 3 — 3 — 3 — 3 — 3 + 3 — 3 — 3 +. R 12 — 3 — 3 — 3 — 3.
  C 3 + 3 + 3 + 3 + 3 + 3 + 3 + 3 — 3 +. R 9 + 3 — 3 — 3.
  C 3 + 3 — 3 + 3 — 3 — 3 — 3 — 3 + 3 +. Tie ends and cut.

Row 4: R 3 × 8. C 3 × 8. R 3 + 3 — 3 — 3 + 3 + 3 — 9. C 3 + 3.
  R 9 + 3 + 3 + 3 — 9. C 3. R 9 + 3 + 3 + 3 — 9. C 3.
  R 9 + 3 + 3 + 3 — 9. C 3 — 3. R 9 + 3 + 3 + 3 — 3 — 3 — 3.
  R 3 × 8. C 3 + 3 + 3 + 3 — 3 — 3 — 3 — 3 +. R 3 × 8.
  C 3 + 3 × 9 +. R 3 × 8. C 3 + 3 — 6 — 3.
  Shuttle 1: R 6 + 3 + 3 — 3 — 3 — 6.
  Shuttle 2: C 3.
  Shuttle 1: R 6 + 3 — 3 — 3 — 3 — 6.
  Shuttle 2: C 3.
  Shuttle 1: R 6 + 3 — 3 — 3 — 3 — 3 — 3 — 6 (the tip).
  Shuttle 2: C 3.
  Shuttle 1: R 6 + 3 — 3 — 3 — 3 — 6.
  Shuttle 2: C 3.
  Shuttle 1: R 6 + 3 — 3 — 3 — 3 — 6.
  Shuttle 2: C 3 + 6 + 3 — 3 +.
  Shuttle 1: R 3 × 8.
  Shuttle 2: C 3 + 3 + 3 — 3 — 3 — 3 — 3 — 3 — 3 +. R 3 × 8.
  C 3 + 3 — 3 — 3 — 3 — 3 — 3 — 3 +. R 3 + 3 — 3 — 3 + 3 + 3 — 9.

There is an illustration of the completed crown on the next page.

Laundering

Tatted lace needs careful handling. It can be boiled in a saucepan, but should not be stirred or scrubbed. After rinsing thoroughly, lay it between two towels, and let it almost dry.

Then pin the lace to something flat, like an ironing board, with a clean towel underneath it. Use rustless pins, sticking one into each loop; this takes time, but it is well worth the trouble. After the lace is dry, it can be ironed, in which case it should be covered by a thin cloth.

Bridal crowns should be starched and put around a bottle of the same size to dry. When they are taken off they will keep their shape and firmness.